Texas Tour Guide

An Enchanting Tourist Guide to Exploring the Beauty, Art, Must-See Attractions, Shopping, Culture and Cuisines in Lone Star State.

Roam Wright

Texas Tour Guide

Copyright © 2023, Roam Wright, All rights reserved.

Texas Tour Guide

TABLE OF CONTENT

MAP OF TEXAS	**6**
INTRODUCTION	**7**
CHAPTER 1	**9**
WELCOME TO TEXAS	9
Historical Background	10
Texan Ingenuity	13
Weather	14
Best Time to Visit Texas	15
What to Wear	15
Culture	17
Language	18
Currency	18
Time	19
Electricity	19
Communications	19
Duty-free	20
Emergency	20
CHAPTER 2	**21**
FAMOUS ATTRACTIONS IN HOUSTON	21
The Museum of Fine Arts	23
The Houston Museum of Natural Science	25
The Houston Zoo	26
The Menil Collection	27

The Houston Children's Museum	29
Gerald D. Hines Waterwall Park	30
Houston's Street Art	31
The Holocaust Museum Houston	32
The Health Museum	34
The McGovern Centennial Gardens	36
BAPS Shri Swaminarayan Mandir	37
Things To Do In Houston	37
CHAPTER 3	**43**
TOP ATTRACTIONS IN DALLAS	43
The Sixth Floor Museum at Dealey Plaza	44
John F. Kennedy Memorial Plaza	46
The Dallas Arboretum and Botanical Garden	47
Dallas World Aquarium	48
Reunion Tower	49
Perot Museum of Nature and Science	50
Klyde Warren Park	52
The Dallas Zoo	52
Bishop Arts District	53
Frontiers of Flight Museum	54
African American Museum	55
Westcave Preserve	56
Grapevine Lake	56
CHAPTER 4	**57**
SAN ANTONIO'S BEAUTIFUL ATTRACTIONS	57
Garden of Japanese Tea	60
National Historic Park of the Missions	62
Yanaguana Garden	64

The Alamo	66
The River Walk	68
Water Adventures	70
CHAPTER 5	**72**
TEXAS BEACHES	72
South Padre Island	72
Galveston	73
The Rockport Beach	75
CHAPTER 6	**77**
CUISINES	77
Tex-Mex	77
BBQ	79
Restaurants	81
Street Foods	85
CHAPTER 7	**89**
HOTELS	89
Luxury Hotels	89
When on a Budget	91
CHAPTER 8	**94**
ANTIQUES AND THRIFT SHOPS	94
CHAPTER 9	**98**
IMPORTANT TIPS	98
CONCLUSION	**102**

Texas Tour Guide

MAP OF TEXAS

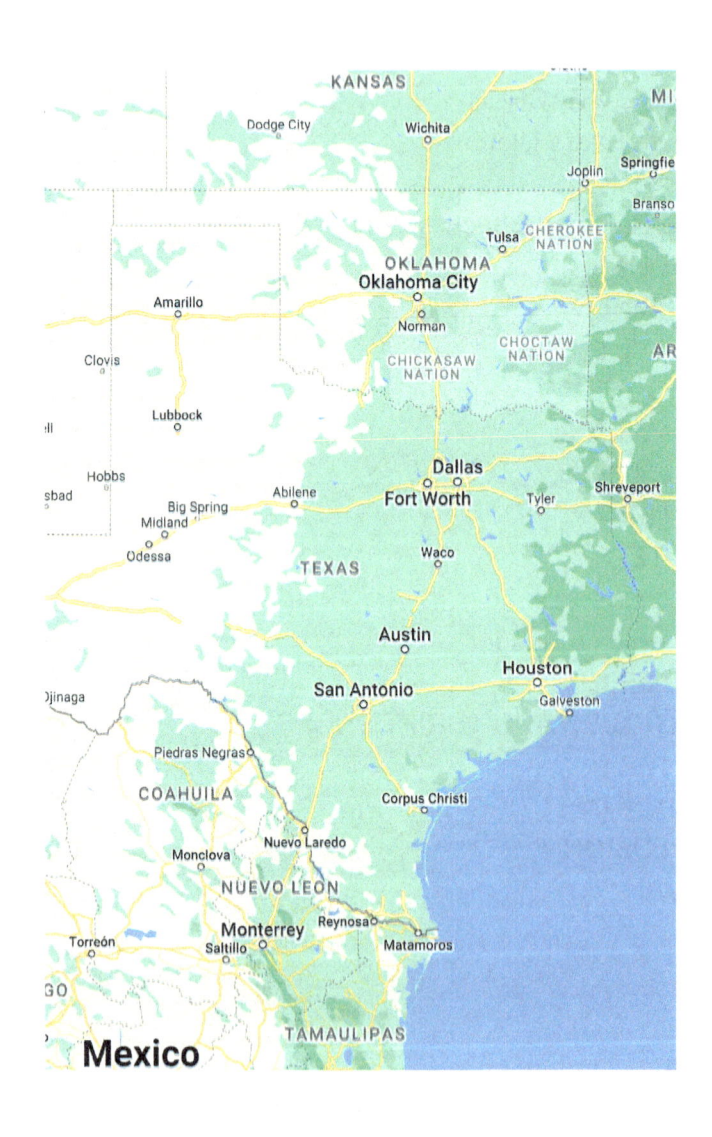

Texas Tour Guide

INTRODUCTION

Welcome to Texas! With its diverse terrain and vibrant culture, Texas offers visitors a wealth of experiences. From exploring the iconic cities of Austin, San Antonio, Dallas, and Houston, to traversing the Texas Hill Country, there are endless opportunities for adventure. From stunning natural parks and awe-inspiring outdoor activities, to tantalizing cuisine and world-class museums, there's something to explore for everyone.

This Texas travel guide provides an overview of the state's many attractions and provides tips on how to make the most of your visit. From exploring Big Bend National Park or tubing the Guadalupe River, you'll find something to do that suits your interests, your Texas travels are sure to be filled with unforgettable moments. So, put on your cowboy boots, and get ready to explore the Lone Star State!

CHAPTER 1

WELCOME TO TEXAS

Texas City is an incredibly vibrant and diverse city, located in the coastal state of Texas. Spanning more than 500 miles in diameter, it is home to a wide variety of attractions and activities to feed the curiosity of any visitor. Its culture is rich with history, its weather warm and inviting, its currency diversified, and its time zone convenient for any traveler.

With its vast array of outdoor activities, exciting festivals, delicious cuisine, and picture-perfect views, it's no wonder why Texas City has been on the must-visit list of travelers for years.

In this chapter, we'll explore the basics of Texas City, highlighting its weather, currency, history, time, and when the best time to visit is. Let's dive right in!

Historical Background

Texas is America's second-biggest and most populous state. It has a complex and multi-cultural past, with a population of Native Americans, Spaniards, Mexicans, Americans, and Anglo-Saxons. It is known for country music, BBQs, cattle ranches, and scorching summers, and is nicknamed the "Lone Star State" due to its battle for independence.

Many Native American tribes lived in America long before Europeans arrived. Texas was home to various indigenous peoples, each with their own distinct culture.

In the east, there existed the Caddo Nation, which grew grain and sunflowers. The Karankawa people lived on the Gulf Coast and were skilled at fishing and building dugout boats. The Comanche, the major tribe in the northwest, were riders and hunters. The Apaches lived in the south and southwest, in teepees and wigwams.

In 1519, the first Spanish explorers landed in Texas. The coastline was charted by Alonso lvarez de Pineda, and afterward Alvar Nez Cabeza de Vaca was shipwrecked off the shore. He spent time with the Native Americans and wrote back to his people, finally persuading the conquistadors to set ships in pursuit of gold (which they never discovered).

After the first explorers landed on the shores, Texas remained essentially unspoiled for around 150 years. Before the Spanish, the French occupied Texas. In 1685, René-Robert Cavelier, Sieur de La Salle, also known as Robert de la Salle, founded Fort St. Louis. The Spanish, on the other hand, were more "successful."

They proceeded to build missions to preach their views, and in 1718, the Misión San Antonio de Valero, often known as The Alamo, was founded. From 1690 to 1821, Texas was a province of Spain.

Texas experienced turbulent periods in the 1800s as it fell under numerous regimes and fought for freedom. Mexico achieved independence from Spain in 1821, and "Tejas" became a part of Mexico. With the consent of the Mexican government, Mexico's open immigration policy drew a large number of Americans to settle in Texas beginning in 1882, led by Stephen Austin and 300 families.

The settlers were not satisfied with adopting the Mexican identity and considered themselves "Texans." They spread fast and far outnumbered Mexicans in Texas. Mexico, fearful of losing authority, promoted increased Mexican immigration and barred immigration from the United States in 1830.

This infuriated the Texans, who launched a revolt and declared independence in 1836. Texas was still under Mexican attack, and while some desired to remain independent, the leaders finally chose to incorporate into the United States of America. Texas became the 28th state in 1845. This resulted in economic growth and the subsequent establishment of the first railroad in 1853 and the first telegraph office in 1854.

However, that was hardly the end of the unrest. Texas left the Union in 1861 to join the Confederacy before returning to the Union in 1870.

The oil boom began in 1901, following the unexpected discovery of oil in Corsicana in 1894. Hughes Tool Company's introduction of the rotating rock drill bit in

1933 aided it. Before it, Texas' principal businesses were cattle and bison, cotton, and lumber.

Texas has a history of a battle for independence as well as inventiveness. The six flags flying above Texas signify the six nations that formerly had jurisdiction over the state: Spain, France, Mexico, the Republic of Texas, the Confederacy, and the United States of America.

Texan Ingenuity

The history of Texas is not only about who reigns and when, but also about the different inventions that originated from the state, ranging from ranching to oil drilling to scientific and technological achievements. For example, Jack Kilby was the first person to show an integrated circuit. He did so in a Dallas laboratory in 1958.

Texas produced condensed milk, as well as the world's first domed and air-conditioned sports stadium and the first mechanical heart implantation. Willie Nelson rose to prominence as a country music superstar, while Doyle Brunson controlled the poker tables with Texas Hold 'em. Both were born in 1933 and wore hats.

Weather

Average temperatures of 30-50 F (about 0-10 C) in winter and 70-90 F (20-30 C) in summer do not vary substantially across the state, but humidity and elevation have a significant impact on comfort. Because Central Texas, East Texas, the Coastal Prairie, and the Rio Grande Valley are humid and close to sea level, it is normally quite hot and sticky in the summer, with temperatures frequently topping 100 degrees Fahrenheit (38 degrees Celsius) between May and October.

Although it does not generally snow or ice in these places, it does happen on occasion. It is very uncommon for places as far south as Austin and San Antonio to get coated with snow, effectively closing down businesses and roadways for the period.

In the Panhandle and higher elevations of the Davis Mountains, Guadalupe Mountains, and Big Bend area, where fall arrives earlier than in the southern part of the state, there is little humidity except for snow, which is common in the winters and sometimes closes roads and mountain areas to the public.

Best Time to Visit Texas

"Tornado Alley" passes through the state, with peak tornado season lasting from late spring to early summer.

Annual rainfall ranges from 8-16 inches (20-40 cm) in the arid Big Bend region to more than 48 inches (122cm) in the state's wettest areas, including Houston and East Texas.

The greatest months for statewide travel are late October/early November, March and April, and late May/early June. This will miss much of Texas's hottest and coldest temperatures, as well as the heaviest rains.

What to Wear

Cotton, linen, and wool are the most comfortable textiles for apparel in the Texas environment. Summer clothing should be light, although due to fluctuating altitude and chilly gusts, a sweater may be required in the evening.

Midwinter in Central and East Texas, the Coastal Prairie, and the Rio Grande Valley normally only needs a light coat. Winters in the Alps, High Plains, and Panhandle may be brutal, necessitating layers of thick clothing.

Texans are relatively casually dressed, and blue jeans are the standard outside of the office. They may be dressed up or down by changing a shirt, sweater, jacket, or accessories and can be worn practically any place, at any time of day. For certain nighttime occasions, people in Dallas and Houston dress formally, while casual slacks and dresses for women and shirt-sleeved or tieless shirts and jackets for men are accepted practically everywhere.

Western attire, with a few exceptions, is casual and aimed toward practical clothes for enjoying the outdoors. Jeans or trousers, polo or button-down shirt, and cowboy boots or shoes are suitable for all but the most formal settings and events. In the warmer months, though, shorts and light shirts are appropriate for most settings.

Wear sunscreen with an SPF of at least 30, polarized eye protection, a broad-brimmed hat (cowboy hats are optional but very useful) to protect your head and neck, layered clothing with sleeves and legs that can be rolled down for sun protection, and sturdy hiking footwear that secures the foot for walking on the rough ground all year long. Flip flops are good for the beach, but you won't want them if you're going to be doing a lot of walking anywhere.

When hiking, use a thin inner polypropylene sock and a thick outer sock to keep your feet dry and comfy. Blisters and painful places can form fast. Cover them with moleskin or medical tape, which is widely available at pharmacies and camping supply stores. Bring a warm coverup and a rain shell; even in the summer, the weather in the high hills may be chilly and unexpected.

Culture

Texan culture is famed for its unwavering belief that everything is bigger and better in Texas. Texan swagger is a genuine social feature, although it is more fun than bothersome. The people of Texas are tremendously proud of their country and fiercely protect every part of it. This is most likely because Texas had to struggle hard to wrest control of its current area from Mexico.

Cowboys make up a significant part of Texan society, thus it's difficult to go across the state without seeing cowboy boots, hats, and rancher attitudes. The majority of pubs play country Western music, and the majority of meals include meat. To a significant extent, everything is bigger in Texas, which is what makes vacationing here so enjoyable. It's a lively, occasionally raucous, yet welcoming state. They're a lot of fun if you get over the fact that Texans think they're the finest thing since sliced bread. The state also has a significant Hispanic population, which provides a nice touch of diversity to the scenery.

Language

Even though Texas does not have an official language, English (particularly, American English) is used for legislation, laws, presidential orders, treaties, education, federal court judgments, and all other official announcements. Due to the significant number of ethnic Mexicans and other Hispanics (Puerto Ricans, Guatemalans, Colombians, etc.), Texas is one state where Spanish is almost as common as English. Some people speak with a faint Texan accent, although it's not widespread.

Currency

The US dollar (US$) is the currency of Texas. Banknotes are available in denominations of $1, $5, $10, $20, $50, and $100. US$1 is made up of 100 cents, with coins in denominations of 1, 5, 10, and 25 cents. Travelers who need to convert money can do it at any of the major cities' banks.

This is also an excellent location to locate ATMs that accept foreign cash cards. Few establishments in Texas refuse to take major credit cards such as Visa and MasterCard.

Time

Texas is largely in the Central Time Zone (GMT -6, GMT -5 during daylight savings between March 12 and November 4).

Electricity

The voltage in Texas is 110-120V/60Hz. Flat two-prong plugs are usual, so carry a universal plug adaptor if you are traveling from Europe or Asia.

Communications

The United States calling code is +1. Texas has many area codes, but the most common are 210 (San Antonio), 214 and 974 (Dallas), and 281 and 783 (Houston). Because of the state's flat landscape, mobile phone service is fairly strong throughout. Any municipality should have no trouble obtaining reception. Wi-Fi hotspots are ubiquitous in coffee shops, libraries, and hotel lobbies, and Internet access is freely available in most large cities.

Duty-free

Everyone over the age of 18 who arrives in America is permitted to bring one liter of alcohol, 200 cigarettes (or 50 non-Cuban cigars or two kilos of tobacco), and $400 in presents without paying customs tax.

Emergency

911 is the number for emergency assistance.

CHAPTER 2

FAMOUS ATTRACTIONS IN HOUSTON

This city is full of diverse attractions for tourists from all over the world. With its cultural and entertainment centers, historical sites, museums, outdoor activities, and many more, tourists can find something to enjoy in this great city. In this chapter, we'll discuss the various attractions for tourists to experience in Houston, so come along and explore what this great city has to offer.

Space Center Houston

Texas Tour Guide

The official visitor center of NASA's Johnson Space Center, Space Center Houston, is a must-see sight in Houston. This is a massive facility where you can go into the replica space shuttle Independence and the massive shuttle carrier aircraft it's installed on.

Inside the visitor center, you may go through a facsimile of America's first space station, Skylab, and touch a moon rock. This is also where you may learn about NASA's prospective projects, such as Mars exploration. On a Friday at noon, you could even get to meet an astronaut.

You may take an open-air tram journey from the visitor center to Johnson Space Center, the headquarters of mission control, to witness where astronauts prepare for space missions. This tour also includes a visit to Rocket Park, where you can view genuine rockets on exhibit. There is no price if you merely want to visit Rocket Park. Simply drive up to the guarded gate, tell them you want to visit, and they will let you in.

Sign up for a Level 9 Tour and get a behind-the-scenes peek at Johnson Space Center for an unforgettable experience. You may see the Buoyancy Lab, ISS Mission Control, and simulation labs, as well as other locations not accessible on ordinary tours, and you may even meet an astronaut. This is a once-in-a-lifetime opportunity, with just 12 tickets available every day for this four- to five-hour VIP tour. Tours begin at the Space Center Houston, which you may visit for free with the purchase of this ticket.

Address: 1601 Nasa Pkwy, Houston, Texas

The Museum of Fine Arts

Houston's Museum of Fine Arts is one of the best museums of its sort in the country. The 63,000 piece collection is divided between two structures: the Audrey Jones Beck Building and the Caroline Wiess Law Building, which are linked by the unusual and remarkable Wilson Tunnel.

The museum's primary collection includes French and Italian Impressionist Renaissance paintings, excellent sculptures, and European and American decorative arts. Check out the incredible collection of gold pre-Columbian and African artifacts.

If you want to explore at your own leisure, there's plenty to keep you engaged and entertained here; but, if it all seems a little overwhelming, sign up for a tour to see the highlights.

If you happen to be near the River Oaks neighborhood, the Bayou Bend and Collections is a satellite gallery that showcases furniture, decorative arts, and paintings.

Houston, Texas, 1001 Bissonnet Street

The Houston Museum of Natural Science

The Houston Museum of Natural Science is one of the city's most popular museums. The museum is a delightful adventure for all ages and covers a wide range of themes that are likely to interest everyone at your party.

During your stay, stop by the Hall of Paleontology to see numerous entire dinosaur skeletons. Tour the Cockrell Butterfly Conservatory, where approximately 1,500 of these lovely butterflies flit around in the humid air, and if you're lucky, one could even land on you.

After learning about what's in the night sky over Houston at the Planetarium, relax your legs and stimulate your senses in the Wortham Giant Screen Theater.

Houston, Texas, 5555 Hermann Park Drive.

The Houston Zoo

The Houston Zoo, located on 55 acres in Hermann Park, is a popular destination for both residents and visitors. The zoo is home to about 6,000 exotic and native species, as well as an education center and a children's zoo. Feeding the giraffes, witnessing marine life up close at the aquarium, and watching sea lions and otters play are all highlights.

Hermann Park also has the Houston Museum of Natural Science, the Miller Outdoor Theatre, a Japanese Garden, and the McGovern Centennial Garden. A paddle boat ride on McGovern Lake or a stroll along the park's walking trails are also enjoyable.

Houston, Texas, 6200 Hermann Park Drive

The Menil Collection

The structure that shelters the Menil Collection is almost as much of a work of art as the objects it houses. The structure, designed by famous architect Renzo Piano, is light-filled thanks to enormous glass windows that look out into the pristine gardens. Unlike many art museums, the art in many (but not all) of the rooms is displayed utilizing natural light.

The Menil Collection is particularly well-known for housing the world's greatest collection of Max Ernst works. Furthermore, the Menil Collection houses modern works of art as well as masterworks in the Byzantine, Abstract, and Surrealism themes. All of these sculptures are shown in their own rooms.

If the weather permits, spend some time exploring the Menil Collection's campus. The Rothko Chapel, with its mural canvases, is one of the most intriguing things to view.

The museum is free to enter.

Houston, Texas (1533 Sul Ross Street)

Texas Tour Guide

The Houston Children's Museum

The Houston Children's Museum is a terrific way to fight the summer heat and one of the greatest places to visit in Houston for families. This vibrant, boisterous environment is sure to put a grin on everyone's face. Allow the youngsters to run wild and get busy with all of the hands on and interactive displays.

The How Does It Work exhibit is a key draw. You and your children will discover how things work in everyday life here. The FlowWorks wet zone is also an intriguing spot where you may switch the water on and off, alter the flow, and observe the results.

Send your kids to the SECRETS Spy Game exhibit if they've ever wanted to pretend to be secret spies. They will use their abilities to crack codes and find clues while competing against malevolent people.

Gerald D. Hines Waterwall Park

The Gerald D. Hines Waterwall Park has a multi-story sculptural fountain with sheets of water falling over enormous concrete walls and sculptures. The semi-circular form of the construction soars 64 feet above you and is framed by a wide arch and 46,500 square feet of water.

Photos do not do this attraction justice; they must be seen in person to be fully understood. This 2.77-acre park in Uptown Houston is shaded by hundreds of live oaks.

Houston's Street Art

While it is sometimes missed by tourists, Houston's street art, also known as graffiti, is excellent. Installations by some of the biggest names in street art from across the world, such as COPE2 and Houston's own Gonzo247, may be found here.

These vibrant murals cover the walls of businesses across the city and are definitely worth taking the time to drive around and see. The flamboyant artist known as Gonzo247 is the unofficial curator of Houston's street art. He is one of the city's most well-known street painters, having created the massive "Houston is Inspired" painting at the intersection of Travis and Preston Streets, as well as the smaller "Houston" artwork at Leeland and St. Emanuel Streets.

This latter region also has a high concentration of stunning installations that adorn the walls of various one- and two-story buildings off Leeland Street between Chartres and St. Emanuel Streets. However, artwork may be seen all around the city on varied-sized walls.

The Holocaust Museum Houston

The Holocaust Museum Houston, which opened in 1996, is the fourth biggest in the US and is located in the Museum District. The museum, which includes various rooms and exhibits depicting the lives of Holocaust victims, strives to teach visitors about hatred, violence, and prejudice.

The museum opens in 2019 following a large 30-million-dollar expansion. The Holocaust Museum Houston is now 57,000 square feet in size, with a 187-seat indoor theater, a 175-seat outdoor amphitheater, and a café.

Interesting anecdotes from survivors, as well as exhibits, are artfully presented in four galleries in an entertaining and thought-provoking manner. The museum houses an authentic railway used to carry victims, as well as a Dutch fishing boat used to transport escapees. Two other galleries house a steady stream of temporary shows.

Address: 5401 Caroline Street, Houston, Texas.

The Health Museum

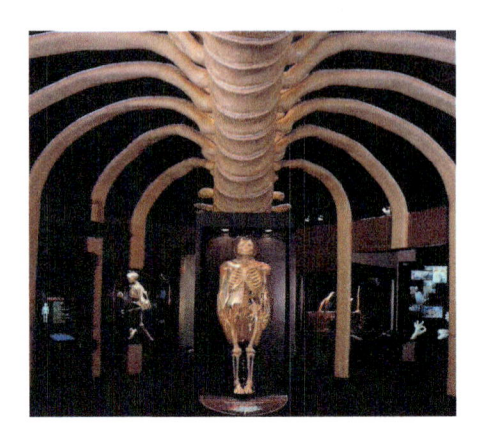

If you've been indulging in Texas' amazing food and are wondering if it's caused your jeans to be a little too tight when you put them on, a visit to the Health Museum is in order. You may practically walk inside your own body at one of Houston's most creative museums.

Walking through a 10-foot-high brain, discovering a 12-foot-high pumping heart, and getting up close and personal with a big eyeball are all enjoyable for the whole family. With the Calorie Crank, you can see how many calories you've consumed when visiting Texas' best BBQ joints!

Houston, Texas (1515 Hermann Drive)

Art Car Museum

If Impressionists and Old Masters paintings aren't your things, check out the Paintings Car Museum. Cars of all types are employed as the medium for unique and unusual artworks in this section. Additionally, frequent pieces of art involving automobiles are shown on exhibition walls.

Since its inception in 1998, the Art Car Museum, commonly known locally as the Garage Mahal, has been a popular Houston attraction. The automobiles and displays change often, and you never know what you'll see as artists try to make something mundane into a distinctive statement or message.

140 Heights Boulevard in Houston, Texas

The McGovern Centennial Gardens

The McGovern Centenary Gardens debuted in 2014 to mark Hermann Park's centenary and rapidly became a popular weekend destination for residents. The fenced-in 8-acre gardens have over 500 trees, 55,000 floral plants, and an educational "edible" garden with fresh food and herbs.

A man-made hill in the center of the gardens leads to the summit through a spiraling trail. Visitors may make the short hike to a tiny observation platform that overlooks the park and see the gardens from a different perspective. The area is ideal for bringing a picnic, taking photographs, and getting some fresh air inside the city.

BAPS Shri Swaminarayan Mandir

The BAPS Shri Swaminarayan Mandir in Houston, completed in 2004, is a prominent Hindu temple designed on Shilpa Shastra principles. The state's biggest, it includes an open-air temple, a haveli, a surrounding deck, open grounds, and an Understanding Hinduism display.

Things To Do In Houston

Walk, Bike, or Paddle in Buffalo Bayou Park
Buffalo Bayou Park is a lovely 160-acre natural park that runs across the city and has the slow-moving waters of

Buffalo Bayou as its focal point. This urban park features miles of walking and bicycling routes, a dog park, sculptures, and lots of shaded spots to unwind.

Rent a kayak, canoe, or stand-up paddleboard and enjoy a paddle down the bayou if you're seeking exciting things to do in Houston, especially if you want to go outside. The park has rentals available, as well as trips ranging from one to three hours in duration. Similarly, guided bike trips are offered by city outfitters.

The Cistern, a historic subterranean drinking-water reservoir from 1926 that currently features changeable art exhibits, is a particularly unusual feature of Buffalo Bayou Park. Visitors can now have a brief guided tour.

The park also has a large colony of Mexican free-tailed bats that live under the Waugh Drive Bridge. Every evening at dusk, around 250,000 of them fly off from the bridge.

Participate in the Houston Livestock Show and Rodeo

The Houston Livestock Show and Rodeo is a fun-filled, 19-day event that gets the entire city out to celebrate every

February or March. If you happen to be in town around this period, you're in luck, and if you're wondering when to visit Houston, now could be the time to do it. This is a fun activity for the whole family that is much more than a rodeo and cattle show.

If this is your first time attending an event of this type, you will be pleasantly surprised by the variety of activities available. There are carnival rides, games, and food vendors on the grounds, as well as enough entertainment to keep you entertained endlessly. Cowboys show off their abilities in several categories at rodeo events, which need tickets to attend. Some of the biggest names in music play on stage in the evening. Check out the musical schedule ahead of time and buy your tickets.

Spend a morning or afternoon wandering the grounds and enjoying the carnival, then see some of the finest farm animals on display at the Livestock Show, then watch a rodeo event or two to see the cowboys in action, and spend the evening at a concert if you only have one day to attend this fantastic show. The Downtown Rodeo Parade is another must-see event.

Take a Stroll Around the Rice University Campus

The Rice University Campus is a downtown Houston oasis and a popular outdoor location for many Houstonians. This 300-acre property features walking and jogging routes, hundreds of mature trees, and charming ancient buildings.

A significant number of stunning contemporary artworks are also on the grounds, adding to the serene mood. Many of these projects are just as spectacular in the evening, if not more so.

Miller Outdoor Theatre

Miller Outdoor Theatre hosts a variety of entertainment from March through October, ranging from concerts to stage shows and movie screenings, and tickets are always free. Even if you don't get a stadium seat, you can always spread a blanket on the hill above the stage and watch the show.

The theater has undergone several restorations since its inception over a century ago, but the famous peaked roof remains a fixture in Houston's busy Hermann Park. Every summer, the theater collaborates with the Houston

Symphony to present the Summer Symphony Nights event, which has been an annual ritual at Miller for decades and is a local favorite.

Explore Houston's underground tunnel network

Exploring North America's biggest subterranean tunnel system, located right in (or should we say beneath) the center of Houston, is never a bad idea when led by a knowledgeable local.

The intricate network of tunnels spans more than 7.5 miles, linking a slew of Houston's busiest business structures.

Guests taking walking tours of the region will learn about Houston's fascinating history and experience firsthand how the objectives of these bunkers have changed over time.

Watch an NBA game at the Toyota Center

Toyota Center, home of the NBA's Houston Rockets, radiates a clamor and energy rivaled by just a few venues in the country.

Outside of basketball season (and even within), the center features sellout concerts by artists such as Harry Styles and Eric Clapton, WWE events, UFC fights, and much more.

Take a day trip to Galveston

Galveston, which is bordered on both sides by the Gulf of Mexico, emanates a bustling coastal environment.

If you're arranging your own trip, start by stretching your legs with a stroll down Pleasure Pier, which is home to a variety of eateries and amusement rides. Following that, Galveston Island State Park is an excellent location for hiking and fishing.

The trip from Houston to Galveston Island should take around an hour, making it an ideal day vacation. You may, however, skip the hassles of traveling, parking and organizing by joining a pre-planned day excursion (or a midnight ghost-themed adventure!).

CHAPTER 3

TOP ATTRACTIONS IN DALLAS

This vibrant and exciting city offers a wide array of must-see attractions for tourists to experience. From world-class art museums and majestic landmarks to the live music scene and incredible shopping attractions, Dallas truly has something for everyone. From classic Texas attractions to cutting-edge technology, Dallas has it all. In this chapter, we'll explore some of the city's top attractions, so buckle up for an incredible journey!

Dallas has a rich history steeped in ranching, farming, and oil production, and it grew swiftly as a commerce hub after the railroad was introduced in 1873. Following WWII, the city became home to major insurance organizations and banks, transforming it into an important commercial and financial center – ideal fodder for the most renowned soap operas about power, money, and intrigue, Dallas.

People visit Dallas for a variety of reasons, including its intriguing history, but there are also several additional attractions and activities to do. The finest area to begin a visit is in the city center. There are several fantastic museums, restaurants, and hotels in the area, as well as other entertaining things to do.

The Sixth Floor Museum at Dealey Plaza

Visitors to the museum are initially exposed to the historical setting through multimedia exhibits that illustrate the political environment of the early 1960s before moving on to emphasize President Kennedy's November 1963 trip to Texas and the final days of his life. Just past here is the sniper's position in the corner window from which Oswald fired the fatal rounds, which has been rebuilt to resemble the original crime scene images.

The remaining exhibitions take you through the chaotic hours after the incident. These include recollections of the nation's and the world's shock, the subsequent investigations, and JFK's legacy.

Historical relics such as a copy of the Mannlicher-Carcano rifle discovered at the crime site, the scale model of Dealey Plaza used by FBI agents throughout the inquiry, forensic evidence, and memorabilia such as Lee Harvey Oswald's wedding band and Jack Ruby's cap are also on display.

Spend some time roaming around Dealey Plaza outside. It's a dramatic experience to view the actual areas of historical significance, such as The Grassy Knoll and roadside signs marking where the fatal gunfire hit John F. Kennedy.
Address: 411 Elm Street in Dallas, Texas

John F. Kennedy Memorial Plaza

The John F. Kennedy Memorial Plaza is just a few streets away from Dealey Plaza, across from the municipal courtroom. This enormous yet simple memorial to President John F. Kennedy was built by famous architect Philip Johnson and finished in 1970 after years of dispute.

The open tomb proposal, which resembled a cenotaph, was intended by Johnson to reflect Kennedy's free spirit. It's a striking sight, standing 30 feet tall and 50 feet broad and built of massive marble slabs. Read the two epitaphs positioned at the monument's entrances; they include a thought-provoking memorial of the President.

Address: 646 Main Street in Dallas, Texas

With a short walk in between, you may see both Dealey Plaza and the memorial on the same visit.

The Dallas Arboretum and Botanical Garden

The Dallas Arboretum and Botanical Garden is located on 66 acres along the southeast bank of White Rock Lake, only minutes from downtown Dallas. The fourteen world-famous exhibits on the grounds feature seasonal flowers, decorative shrubs, trees, and plant collections. Seasonal outdoor festivals, concerts, art displays, and educational events are also held at the grounds, and guided tours of the area are offered.

Despite being envisaged in the early 1930s, this magnificent tourist attraction did not become a reality until 1984, when it was erected on the grounds of a home completed in 1939. The magnificent sculptures and fountains in sections such as Toad's Corner, Texas Town, and Pecan Grove add to the excitement.

Make time to explore the area around White Rock Lake Park as well. This massive lake encompasses an area of over 1,000 acres and is recognized for its great bird and wildlife viewing, as well as fishing and sailing adventures. It is surrounded by 10 miles of hiking and bike paths.

Address: 8525 Garland Road, Dallas, Texas

Dallas World Aquarium

Dallas World Aquarium is a pleasant and instructive experience for young and old alike, conveniently located within easy walking distance of the city's historic downtown center. A diverse range of sea life, including bonnethead sharks, stingrays, jellyfish, sea turtles, gigantic groupers, and rare leafy seadragons, is housed in 87,000 gallons of saltwater.

The Orinoco Rainforest display is a wonderful feature. This entertaining attraction has several free-flying birds such as toucans, as well as tree sloths and aquatic species such as Orinoco crocodiles and poison dart frogs. Check the feeding schedule before you arrive to see the animals at their most energetic, as well as for information on future seminars and lectures.

Plan to eat at one of the aquarium's three restaurants, which provide anything from gourmet and international cuisine to sandwiches and snacks with views of the local aquatic life.

Address: Dallas, Texas, 1801 N. Griffin Street

Reunion Tower

While not the highest structure in Dallas, the Reunion Tower is unquestionably the most distinguishing and unmistakable. Its 560-foot length is beautifully lighted up at night, accentuating its distinctive design. It was completed in 1978 and appears as a geodesic ball resting on five cylindrical concrete poles.

The tower's showpiece is the GeO-Deck observation viewing platform, which offers panoramic views of Dallas from 470 feet in the air. From yoga to art courses, there are constantly unique activities going on with those 360-degree vistas.

300 Reunion Boulevard E, Dallas, Texas

Perot Museum of Nature and Science

The Perot Museum of Nature and Science, housed in a gigantic architectural marvel created by Thom Mayne, is a favorite Dallas destination for children and curious travelers.

The building itself was created with sustainability in mind. Summer water saving with recaptured condensation from air conditioners and drip irrigation, the use of recycled and locally produced construction materials, and solar-powered water heaters are among the innovative eco-friendly design elements.

The museum is split into thematic sections that include interactive educational stations, games, and high-tech exhibits. Engineering and innovation, energy, evolution, earth sciences, and other topics are among them. It also has a 3D cinema, the Moody Family Children's Museum and playground, and a 54-foot escalator with a glass box that overlooks the site.

Dallas, Texas (2201 N. Field Street)

Klyde Warren Park

Klyde Warren Park is a nice area to stop and rest as you walk around downtown Dallas. The lovely public park is a haven of calm in the city streets and high-rise buildings. Food trucks, outdoor eating, green space, public art, and a laid-back social environment may all be found on any given day.

There are cafés and several sitting spaces near the fountains around the five-acre park. There are constant public activities at the park, but it's just as enjoyable to bring a blanket and a picnic while you explore the area attractions and find a half hour to relax and enjoy the Dallas city scene.

Dallas, Texas, 1909 Woodall Rodgers Freeway

The Dallas Zoo

The Dallas Zoo is a 106-acre facility that houses almost 2,000 exotic animals from 406 different species in a range of settings. This exciting site, just three miles from the city center, has always been popular with families. It was founded in 1888, making it one of the oldest zoos in the United States.

ZooNorth, the Wilds of Africa, Giants of the Savanna, and a children's zoo are among the geographic regions of the zoo. Animal encounters, such as daily giraffe feedings, presentations on the Wild Encounters Stage, and the interactive aviary Birds Landing are among the most engaging zoo experiences.

While there are various restaurants and snack kiosks on the grounds, you might want to carry a picnic and eat it at one of the picnic tables placed around the zoo grounds.

Dallas, Texas, 650 S R L Thornton Fwy

Bishop Arts District

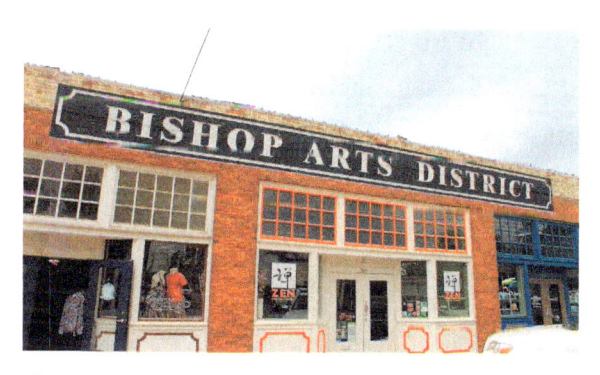

If you're looking for things to do in Dallas, the Bishop Arts District in the North Oak Cliff area boasts practically limitless options for shopping, dining, and entertainment. More than sixty independently owned and run enterprises are represented. Chic boutiques, art galleries, restaurants, and quiet coffee shops abound in this charming small-town setting.

Among the distinctive purveyors are specialty stores catering to male clients, such as the bizarre M'antiques; various women's vintage clothes businesses; and a plethora of shops carrying products manufactured by local artists and designers. The area, which has a strong feeling of community, frequently conducts family-friendly street festivals and public entertainment.

Frontiers of Flight Museum

The Frontiers of Flight Museum houses over 40 aircraft and space vehicles, as well as significant exhibits that trace the history of aviation from Leonardo da Vinci through present space exploration. A full-size model of the Wright Flyer, items from the Hindenburg, and several WWI and WWII aircraft and artifacts are among the museum's outstanding collections.

A completely restored Stearman PT-17 Kaydet Biplane and the Apollo VII spacecraft are among the vintage aircraft on show. The Braniff Gallery and Virgin America exhibit, which are on display at the museum's Love Field facility, illustrate the history of commercial aviation.

6911 Lemmon Avenue, Dallas, Texas

African American Museum

The African American Museum, which opened in 1974, contains a range of exhibitions of African American artistic, cultural, and historical elements. The museum's collection is rich in references to traditional African themes and cultural icons, and it also includes a library and historical archive.

In addition to hundreds of items, the center has sculptures, paintings, and the greatest collection of African American folk art in the United States. The on-site theater also hosts educational and entertaining activities.

Westcave Preserve

Westcave Preserve, a protected area situated in a canyon, contains a fairy-tale-like grotto that may be reached by a short walk surrounded by gorgeous wildlife and canyon walls.

The preserve is available to the public and may be visited via educational and entertaining guided tours (reservations are necessary). It is a one-of-a-kind experience and a Texas natural treasure not to be missed.

Grapevine Lake

The 8,000-acre lake is located in the middle of Dallas-Fort Worth and offers endless outdoor activities. You may camp directly on the water, picnic, sail, motorboat, jet ski, fish, or simply relax on the magnificent granite cliff beach. It has various paths and pathways with beautiful views and varying levels of difficulty.

CHAPTER 4

SAN ANTONIO'S BEAUTIFUL ATTRACTIONS

San Antonio is a city that offers a plethora of attractions for tourists of every interest. From historic landmarks and museums to a wide variety of cultural and entertainment venues, San Antonio has something for everyone.

Art lovers can explore San Antonio's world-renowned museums, while nature-lovers can embark on thrilling outdoor adventures. For those looking for a unique experience, San Antonio has a variety of unique attractions and activities to explore.

In this chapter, we'll explore the various attractions and activities that make San Antonio such a great place to visit.

Natural Bridge Cavern

Natural Bridge Caverns is a cave system located near San Antonio, Texas in the Texas Hill Country. It is the largest commercial cavern known in Texas and one of the largest in the world. Four college students found the natural limestone formation in 1960, and it was introduced to the public in 1966.

The caves are named after a natural limestone bridge that runs under them. Bolted ladders and walkways were installed to assist tourists in navigating the twisting and sometimes treacherous corridors. Stalactites, stalagmites, flowstones, rimstone dams, and columns are among the natural mineral formations found in the cave.

The large "Hall of the Mountain King" center area can house up to 400 people and is well recognized for its spectacular exposed stalactites and multicolored lightning-bug-like mineral formations.

Natural Bridge Caverns excursions are available all year, allowing guests to see a variety of cave attractions up close. The Discovery Tour, which takes tourists through one-third of the cavern, the Hidden Passages Tour, which takes people into otherwise inaccessible tunnels, and the Explorer's Adventure Tour, which is only open to expert cavers, are among the tours available.

A range of family activities and events are also available at the caves. Visitors may zip-line from one balcony to another and tackle an obstacle course on the Explorer's Challenge Ropes Course and Zip Line tour, which debuted in 2015. The Canopy Walk allows guests to see the rest of the cave system from above, while the Panning for Gems experience lets tourists mine for southern Texas gems. Seasonal events such as spelunking and caving explorations are also available.

Natural Bridge Caverns is an official Natural History site that contributes significantly to local tourism. It is a favorite location for educational field excursions, business team building, and any other type of learning adventure.

San Antonio, TX 78266 26610 Natural Bridge Caverns Rd

Garden of Japanese Tea

The Japanese Tea Garden in San Antonio, Texas, is a peaceful haven amid the metropolis. It is a serene hideaway in Brackenridge Park that emulates the traditional serenity of Japan and its beautiful, green gardens.

The Garden was built as part of a Depression-era make-work initiative in the 1930s when Chinese and Japanese immigrants were brought in to build a park. The garden has been transformed into a wonderful location, complete with a walkway of more than 100 stepping stones and the exquisite arches of a Chinese temple. Pebbled pathways run through a beautiful environment of trees, bushes, and flowers, passing by stone lanterns, pagodas, and waterfalls.

Visitors to the Japanese Tea Garden may enjoy the serene ambiance, rest under the trees, or photograph the beautiful koi fish that swim in a huge pond. There are also several tea rooms where guests may relax and ponder while taking in the beauty of the garden. A big Japanese bell that originally hung outside of a temple in Tokyo and was donated to the Garden in the 1980s may be found near the Garden's entrance.

The Japanese Tea Garden is a serene oasis in the center of the city, where visitors may experience nature's tranquility and a history steeped in Japanese culture. The Japanese Tea Garden is the ideal location for a leisurely stroll, a cup of tea, or simply sitting and relaxing.

3853 North St. Mary's Street, San Antonio, Texas 78212

National Historic Park of the Missions

The Missions National Historical Park in San Antonio, Texas, is a well-known destination for both history and wildlife enthusiasts. The park, which spans over 8 acres of land, provides breathtaking views of four of San Antonio's Spanish Missions: Concepción, San José, San Juan, and Espada.

These Missions, built by Franciscan missionaries in the late 1700s and early 1800s, are the oldest and finest preserved

Spanish colonial missions in the United States. The park, which is part of the World Heritage Site of the San Antonio Missions, is one of the most visited historical attractions in the country.

The rich legacy and distinctive architecture of Missions National Historical Park make it a wonderful destination for tourists. Visitors to the Missions may explore the grounds, see the gorgeous architecture, learn about their history, and even visit the surrounding cemetery. The park is an excellent location for photography, and there is a lot of artwork on show inside the grounds.

The park provides tourists with a range of excursions and activities. Visitors may learn more about the Missions and their tales by joining guided tours led by Park Rangers and docents. Tour groups can also visit the neighboring marshes and Pioneer Cemetery, which date back to San Antonio's early Spanish colonization.

Furthermore, throughout the year, the park holds many culturally significant festivities, such as Fiesta San Antonio, which commemorates the city's tricentennial.

Missions National Historical Park, with its magnificent history, culture, and nature, provides a one-of-a-kind experience to tourists of all backgrounds. Visitors will have a remarkable and pleasurable experience whether they visit for a day or spend a weekend exploring the park.

San Antonio, Texas 78214 6701 San José Drive

Yanaguana Garden

Yanaguana Garden is a 4.6-acre public park in downtown San Antonio, Texas, located along the San Antonio River Walk. The park, named after the original meaning of "refreshing waters" in the region's earliest residents'

64

language, serves as a community center for amusement, leisure, and play.

The park offers a range of interactive activities aimed at people of all ages. The park's design, which includes a riverboat-themed playscape, a small amphitheater, and a playground structure replete with a climbing wall, swings, slides, and a huge sandbox, allows all generations to explore, learn, and partake in a unique and vivid interactive experience.

The sprayground, a 6,500-square-foot interactive fountain that employs recirculating pumps to generate varied water patterns and designs, is the park's focal point. Visitors may refresh themselves in the misty spray as families and children of all ages enjoy the play areas.

The experience also has an educational component. Six interactive kiosks, equipped with light-up touchscreens and interactive audio components, exhibit the park's history and ecosystem. There are also two outdoor classrooms, which are ideal for gatherings and learning in a lovely outdoor setting for families, groups, and classes.

Yanaguana Garden, which is open seasonally all year, is a terrific location for families, friends, and locals to congregate, explore, and have fun. Whether it's to cool down in the sprayground or to learn about the ecology of the region, the park in all its splendor offers a magnificent getaway to the calm and beauty of nature in downtown San Antonio.

The Alamo

The Alamo in San Antonio, Texas, is one of America's most famous and historic locations. The Alamo was founded in 1718 by Spanish priests as a mission and stronghold. The Alamo became famous across the world in 1836 when it played a critical part in the Texas Revolution, notably the Battle of the Alamo.

The Alamo is currently part of a 4.2-acre complex that comprises the Alamo grounds, chapel, and Long Barrack, as well as a four-level museum and library. It is a declared United States National Historic Landmark, and over 2.5 million people visit the site each year to memorialize those who gave their lives for the cause of Texas independence.

The Alamo's Chapel is the Alamo's focal point. It is a one-room chapel erected in 1750 that serves as a poignant reminder of the Alamo's defenders and their battle for liberty. Visitors are welcome to visit the chapel and grounds, as well as learn more about its history.

The Long Barrack is located next to the chapel. The Long Barrack, which was built in 1836, was originally utilized as a sanctuary by the Tejanos, local Mexican settlers who assisted Texan soldiers in their war with Mexican forces. It is currently a museum with relics and displays from the fight. Visitors may also walk around the grounds and learn about the Texans who led the revolution.

The Alamo also has a library and museum with a large collection of historical papers, relics, and images linked to the conflict and the Texas Revolution. Visitors can tour the many exhibitions to obtain a better knowledge of the events and people that impacted Texas's history.

The Alamo is one of the most significant historical places in the United States, and it remains a symbol of bravery and persistence. Visitors to the Alamo may respect and remember the warriors who died fighting for freedom in this epic conflict.

San Antonio, TX 78205, 300 Alamo Plaza.

The River Walk

The RiverWalk in San Antonio, Texas, is one of the state's most beautiful attractions. The River Walk, which runs along the banks of the San Antonio River, is known as the "Venice of Texas." Explore the twisting paths that lead past restaurants, stores, galleries, hotels, and gardens. Explore the finest of what San Antonio has to offer by taking a stroll downstream from downtown.

Begin your tour at Rivercenter Mall's Shops. This region, located near the Alamo, offers visitors a plethora of retail opportunities. Explore designer boutiques, bookstores, and souvenir shops, among other things. When you need a break, stop for a bite to eat at one of the numerous local eateries or enjoy a drink at a bar or cafe along the River Walk.

Take some time to explore some of the River Walk's most recognizable sights. Stop at St. Anthony's Bridge, created in 1941 by architect Robert Hugman. Other close attractions include the old Menger Hotel, the Majestic Theatre, and several others. Don't miss the San Antonio Museum of Art, which is nestled beneath the ancient Gran Cenote Bridge.

The River Walk experience would be incomplete without a ride on one of the river's water taxis. Take in the fresh air as you sail by restaurants, hotels, and gardens. Keep an eye out for the various bird species that inhabit the river, which will enhance your boat journey.

San Antonio's River Walk is one of the city's most lovely sights. There is no shortage of fun and adventure to be experienced, from the stores to the numerous other activities. Set aside some time to explore this beautiful location and all it has to offer.

Water Adventures

San Antonio, Texas, has a variety of picturesque and entertaining water tours to see the city and its surroundings. There's something for everyone, from relaxing river excursions to kayaking experiences.

A leisurely boat tour is an excellent way to experience the San Antonio Riverwalk. These sightseeing boat tours transport guests along the San Antonio River, giving them a close-up view of the historic structures and landmarks that border it. Tour guides give excellent comments on the surrounding area as well as the city's history. One-hour tours to afternoon excursions are available aboard cruises.

Visitors looking for a more adventurous water excursion can go kayaking. These excursions take paddlers along the San Antonio River and its environs, letting them observe the area's unique animal and bird species. Professional guides conduct safety briefings and teach beginners the fundamentals of kayaking. Tours range in length from an hour to a whole day.

A mission boat excursion is also an excellent way to get away from the city core. You'll enjoy a leisurely ride down the San

Antonio River, stopping to view the five well-preserved historic Spanish missions in the vicinity. This one-of-a-kind boat excursion mixes history and natural beauty. You may also stop along the way to investigate more thoroughly.

The San Antonio Moonlight Paddleboat Tour is an excellent opportunity to see the city's splendor from a different angle. This evening cruise takes paddlers through the fog and beneath the stars, providing amazing views of the river and the city skyline. It's the ideal way to unwind and take in the sights of San Antonio.

San Antonio also has several lakes and ponds, which visitors may explore with the aid of knowledgeable tour guides. You can appreciate the stunning views while also having a wonderful day out on the water with Jet Ski rentals and guided fishing outings.

Whatever method you choose to explore San Antonio's waterways, these trips provide a unique and fascinating way to do so. You'll find something to suit you, from river cruises to kayak experiences and everything in between.

CHAPTER 5

TEXAS BEACHES

Beaches in Texas have been a popular destination for vacationers and locals alike. From the vast beaches of Galveston and Padre Island to the smaller, quieter beaches of Rockport and Corpus Christi, the Lone Star State has some of the country's best coastlines. In this chapter, we will explore the top Texas beaches, providing information on each destination's unique attractions and activities.

South Padre Island

A barrier island paradise on the gorgeous Gulf Coast's southernmost tip. When you visit South Padre Island, you come for the sun-kissed beaches and crystal blue ocean waters, but you also come for the multitude of sports available, such as fishing, surfing, windsurfing, and kiteboarding.

If you're searching for a beach vacation that's full of fun and excitement, South Padre Island is the place to go! It's a place to rest and unwind, with its pure white sand beaches spanning along the Gulf of Mexico. South Padre Island has something for everyone, from sunbathing to parasailing and jet skiing.

You'll find lots of things to keep you and your family occupied during your visit, whether you're seeking adventure or leisure. South Padre Island has plenty of activities for guests of all ages, whether you want to go dolphin watching or participating in one of the many fishing excursions. Furthermore, for those searching for a good time, the island has lots of shopping, restaurants, and entertainment.

South Padre Island is a destination that should not be missed, from its distinct animals and marshlands to its breathtaking sunsets. Spend some time soaking up the sun and surf, or simply enjoying the island's warmth and beauty. Whatever you choose to do with your stay on South Padre Island, you will have an amazing experience.

Galveston

One of the most thrilling and gorgeous beaches in America. This lovely beach, located about 55 miles southeast of

Houston on the Gulf Coast, is the ideal spot for a fun-filled holiday. Galveston Beach has something for everyone, from breathtaking sunsets to renowned activities.

The beach is one of the most popular sites on the island, with white sand beaches, calm waves, and lots of sunshine, making it ideal for sunbathing, swimming, and participating in water activities like jet skiing, kayaking, and snorkeling. There are also some beachfront hotels and resorts with direct beach access for your convenience.

Galveston Beach also has a lively entertainment center, with a diverse selection of restaurants, pubs, and nightclubs, as well as attractions including the Galveston Island Historic Pleasure Pier and the Moody Gardens Aquarium and Rainforest. Galveston provides something for everyone, whether it's a romantic evening or a night of partying with friends.

Galveston Beach also has some of the greatest fishing in Texas. Enjoy the abundant marine life by taking a day excursion out to the jetty or fishing off one of the numerous piers. Galveston offers a terrific day on the water with everything from perch and catfish to red snapper and deep sea creatures.

To round off your vacation, browse through the historic Strand retail district for one-of-a-kind things and souvenirs, or participate in the fun of Mardi Gras, the city's annual carnival festival. With so much to offer, it's no surprise that Galveston Beach in Texas is a memorable visit.

The Rockport Beach

Rockport Beach is a beach on the Texas Gulf Coast near the small seaside town of Rockport, Texas. Rockport is well-known for its stunning sunsets, pristine beaches, and welcoming residents. This beach is a haven for individuals looking for a calm escape from the stresses of everyday life.

Rockport Beach's white sands spread for kilometers, making it an ideal location for swimming and surfing. The temperature of the offshore waters remains consistent, allowing swimmers to stay cool during the hot months. Winter months are ideal for surfing since the Gulf of Mexico produces larger swells.

Rockport Beach is also known for fishing. Visitors may book charters to experience some of the greatest freshwater and deep-sea fishing in the area. You'll have a great day fishing off the sands of Rockport Beach, whether you're chasing black drum, snapper, or trout.

Visitors can explore surrounding attractions after a day of beach activities. Beautiful 19th-century residences, galleries, restaurants, and stores can be found in historic downtown Rockport. Visitors may enhance their experience by taking the Aransas Queen Bay Cruise, which goes along Rockport Bay and provides spectacular views of seabirds and animals.

Visit Rockport Beach for a genuinely unique experience. Rockport Beach provides something for everyone, whether it's swimming, surfing, fishing, or simply resting.

CHAPTER 6

CUISINES

In this chapter, we'll be taking a look at some of the most popular and iconic cuisines associated with the state: Tex-Mex and barbecue. We'll explore the flavor profiles and ingredients that make Texas-style cuisine so distinctive, as well as the different dishes – from classic plates to street food. For the true foodies, we'll also provide a list of some of the best restaurants to try out for an authentic Texas dining experience whether you're visiting in-person or ordering in from the comfort of home

Tex-Mex

Tex-Mex food is a distinct style of cooking with origins in Mexican and Texan cuisine. It combines components of Mexican cookery with Texas characteristics, such as spices, meat, chile peppers, cheese, and other ingredients. Tex-Mex cuisine has gained popularity in the United States and may be found at a variety of establishments.

Beans, chiles, and spices are the key components of Tex-Mex cookery, while rice is frequently served as a side dish. The burrito is a popular meal in the cuisine, consisting of a flour tortilla filled with refried beans, veggies, cheese, and/or meat and wrapped in a soft tortilla. Enchiladas, tacos, quesadillas, fajitas, and tamales are among popular Tex-Mex foods.

Chili con carne, a spicy beef stew cooked with tomatoes, kidney beans, onion, garlic, and numerous spices, is one of the most popular Tex-Mex recipes. This meal is frequently accompanied by cheddar cheese, sour cream, guacamole, and tortillas. Nachos, another famous food, are created with tortilla chips, cheese, and seasonings.

Fajitas are thin strips of grilled meat, poultry, or vegetables served in a taco shell or tortilla, generally topped with shredded cheese and sour cream. Quesadillas, which are simple wheat or corn tortillas stuffed with cheese and other meats or veggies, are also popular.

Soups and salads can also have Tex-Mex flavors. Salads like taco salad and fajita taco salad are popular, as are soups like tortilla soup and chili with carne. Fresh ingredients are combined with a variety of spices to produce a unique and savory dish that is guaranteed to impress.

Whatever sort of Tex-Mex food you pick, you will have a great and substantial supper. Tex-Mex food is a delicious way to combine Mexican ingredients with Texas influences. So, the next time you're in the mood for something delectable and spicy, consider Tex-Mex cuisine.

BBQ

Texas BBQ is a distinct and delectable kind of barbecue prevalent throughout the Lone Star State. Texas BBQ has been inspired by many different cultures, but its roots may be found in the Southern custom of slow-cooking meats over open wood fires. Texas BBQ is known for its robust and smokey flavor, which is generally achieved by combining mesquite, hickory, and oak woods.

The meats used in Texas BBQ vary by area, although brisket is a traditional choice. Brisket is slow-cooked for many hours, giving it a distinct, smokey taste. Ribs, pig, chicken, and turkey are among the common meats used in Texas BBQ.

Here are some wonderful foods to try if you're visiting Texas and want to sample true Texas BBQ:

1. Brisket: Brisket is a traditional Texas BBQ meat. It's typically accompanied by white bread, pickles, onions, and BBQ sauce.

2. Ribs: Ribs are a tasty and traditional Texas BBQ meal. They're often grilled over a wood fire and served with barbecue sauce.

3. Pulled pork: This meal is typically served with rich BBQ sauce or coleslaw and is cooked low and slow.

4. Sausage: Typically cooked from pig, beef, or turkey, Texas sausage is eaten with a variety of sides.

5. Smoked turkey: To give it a smokey taste, turkey is sometimes smoked with mesquite or hickory.

6. Beef ribs: Served with BBQ sauce, these ribs are grilled over a wood fire.

7. Beef brisket tacos: These tacos are often loaded with shredded beef brisket and served on a soft flour tortilla and are deliciously smokey.

When in Texas, try some of these traditional Texas BBQ meals to get a true taste of the Lone Star State. Enjoy!

Restaurants

- ## Matt's El Rancho

Matt in the background Matt's El Rancho began selling tamales at the age of six in 1923, so you know you're in for some time-tested recipes. Matt's El Rancho has been serving the greatest Tex-Mex and Mexican food in Austin since 1952. Each menu item, from the lava-like queso to the crunchy chicken flautas, is more delectable and savory than the previous. Work your way down the menu, beginning with the bean and cheese nachos.

- ## Mi Tierra Cafe y Panaderia

Mi Tierra has been providing some of the greatest Tex-Mex cuisines in the state for 75 years. Mi Tierra is the place to be whether you want some local mariachi music, an ice-cold marg, sizzling fajitas, or simply some Tejano warmth. This downtown San Antonio favorite serves fajitas, margaritas, and much more.

- **Panchito's**

This neighborhood Tex-Max restaurant is ideal for breakfast, lunch, or supper. Choose from one of their delectable morning tacos, spicy enchiladas, or flawlessly sizzled fajitas. Or, like us, order all three. In either case, you'll have a fantastic supper at Panchito's. It is located in San Antonio.

- **Mia's Tex Mex Restaurant**

This Lemmon Ave treasure is a fixture in Dallas' Tex-Mex culture. Aside from Tex-Mex favorites like smothered burritos and sizzling fajitas, their house brisket tacos and deep-fried chimichangas are to die for. When it comes to fajitas at Mia's, you have to go big or go home, so we recommend the Cowboy Platter, which includes beef, chicken, and shrimp fajitas as well as a heaping helping of rice and beans.

- **Gabriela and Sofia's Tex-Mex in Dallas**

Gabriela & Sofia's Tex-Mex takes pride in serving recipes "stolen right out of mom's kitchen." So you know you're dining in a relaxed and welcoming environment. Every item on their menu is delicious, but the nachos de la casa and chile con queso are legendary.

- **Dallas's Mi Cocina**

Mi Cocina is a tiny North Texas chain that serves the greatest Tex-Mex cuisine. They are among the best in terms of service, modern and cozy atmosphere, and great Tejano cuisine. Begin with any of their nacho platters, such as the nachos locos with picadillo meat, beans, queso, guacamole, and pico de gallo. How about Habana nachos with adobo-smothered chicken?

- **Gloria's Latin Cuisine - Dallas**

Anyone in D-Town will tell you that Gloria's serves the greatest Tex-Mex and Salvadorian food in the city. This

Latin favorite perfectly blends the two cuisines in a cozy yet elegant atmosphere. Treat yourself to their crispy chicken flautas, ceviche tostadas, or stuffed chile rellenos for a supper you won't soon forget.

- **La Fonda On Main**

A tourist and local favorite is located just outside of downtown. La Fonda on Main is the city's oldest Mexican restaurant, so they've had plenty of time to develop all of their greatest dishes. Everything on their menu is delicious, and the ambiance is ideal. On their shady terrace, don't forget to order a couple of blood orange margaritas or ice-cold micheladas. A very good restaurant to stop by in San Antonio.

- **Lopez**

Lopez has been the Houston expert on outstanding Tex-Mex food since 1978. You'll find a fantastic selection of your favorites here, including puffed and crispy chalupas, massive burritos, and crunchy tacos stuffed with ground meat. We recommend the Lopez combination, which includes two cheese enchiladas, a beef taco, a chile con queso puff, and chile relleno.

Street Foods

- Puffy Taco

The puffy taco, which is best characterized as a cross between a funnel cake and a tostada, is a crispy, fried food made in San Antonio by brothers Ray and Henry Lopez. The fluffy taco dough is made from ground corn masa, water, and salt. The dough is flattened in a tortilla press, deep-fried, and then a spoon is inserted into the center of the taco until it coils around it.

Following that, the taco is loaded with items such as carnitas or fried avocados. Eating a puffy taco is a messy affair since it is considered that a truly puffy taco should be oily and crumbly.

- Corn Dog

A corn dog is made of processed beef on a stick that is deep-fried after being dipped in cornmeal batter. It is a very popular snack (and hot dog variant) in the United States of America. Corn dogs are commonly available at county fairs, carnivals, sports arenas, mall food courts, and roadside cafes.

Neil Fletcher popularized this tasty snack at the Texas State Fair in 1942, however, sellers at the Minnesota State Fair say they originated it in 1941 when it was known as a Pronto Pup.

Corn dogs are now commonly eaten with yellow mustard, pickles, sauerkraut, or mayonnaise, and there are other versions of the snack across the world, particularly in Argentina, Australia, New Zealand, and Japan.

- Brisket Sandwich

Succulent, slow-smoked beef brisket is served on a slice of bread or roll with a variety of traditional toppings such as barbeque sauce, pickles, onions, and jalapenos.

- Texas Chili

Tender meat, tomatoes, chili powder, cumin, and a variety of spices make up this hearty dish. On the side, a warm wheat tortilla and grated cheese.

- Loaded Frito Pie

A crispy Frito-filled pleasure labeled "Texas' favorite snack." Filled with meat, beans, chiles, onions, tomatoes, and a generous helping of strong cheddar cheese.

- Texas BBQ

A must-try for every BBQ enthusiast! Delicious homemade sauce and grilled corn on the cob accompany the juicy beef and ribs.

- Fried Green Tomatoes

Sliced green tomatoes are slightly dipped in an egg and milk batter before being seasoned and fried. For dipping, a unique spicy remoulade sauce is served.

- Migas

A traditional South Texas egg meal that consists of scrambled eggs, green bell peppers, onions, melted cheese, and corn tortilla strips.

- Elotes

Grilled Mexican street corn topped with mayonnaise, cotija cheese, chili powder, lime, and cilantro.

- Chicken-fried Steak

A traditional culinary experience consisting of a cube steak covered in a light batter and fried to crisp perfection. Traditional gravy and side items such as mashed potatoes or coleslaw are served.

- Kolaches

A delicious pastry with Czech influences that is filled with cream cheese, fruit, and sugar and wrapped in a delicate, flaky dough.

CHAPTER 7

HOTELS

We have included both luxury and budget hotels to provide you with a wide range of options to suit your preferences and needs. These hotels are just the tip of the iceberg and there are many more just waiting to be discovered. So, no matter how much you are willing to spend on your accommodation, there are a lot of options available to you. As you start your search for the perfect place to stay in Texas, this guide will be your most valuable companion.

Luxury Hotels

1. St. Regis San Antonio: This five-star hotel in downtown San Antonio provides the finest degree of elegance and convenience with its package of facilities. Guests may enjoy a private pool, spa, and fitness center, two rooftop bars, and exceptional dining selections in the three-story restaurant.

2. Rosewood Mansion on Turtle Creek: This historic Dallas property offers boutique-inspired rooms as well as superb service. Enjoy exquisite amenities including marble showers, an outdoor heated pool, two award-winning restaurants, and stylish event spaces.

3. Hotel Emma: This magnificent hotel in San Antonio's historic Pearl Brewery provides farm-to-table food, modern conveniences, and features such as a rooftop pool, a craft cocktail bar, and a spa.

4. The Driskill Hotel: Over the years, this renowned Austin landmark has welcomed various celebrities, statesmen, and performers. Guests may now enjoy contemporary facilities, luxurious lodgings, and family-friendly activities.

5. Four Seasons Hotel Houston: With its art deco architecture, great dining options, an indoor pool, a lavish spa, and smart event spaces, this luxury hotel in Houston provides guests with a contemporary experience.

6. The Ritz-Carlton in Dallas: The Ritz-Carlton: Dallas, which combines historic architecture and modern comforts, offers the best of both worlds. Among the amenities

available to guests are exquisite restaurants, a spa, a pool, and a fitness center.

7. The Lake Austin Spa Resort: Located on the shores of Lake Austin in Austin, this luxury resort provides a relaxing retreat with lakeside cabanas, a variety of spa treatments, and outstanding on-site restaurants.

When on a Budget

These are some of the best hotels to lodge in that will still you you utmost comfort.

1. Hotel Indigo San Antonio Airport: Located near San Antonio International Airport, the Hotel Indigo San Antonio Airport has comfortable accommodations starting at $119 per night. Guests may make use of modern amenities such as a fitness center, an outdoor pool, and complimentary Wi-Fi.

2. Belmont Dallas: With prices starting at $80/night, the Belmont Dallas is an excellent deal. Parking, breakfast, a swimming pool, and on site laundry are all available at the motel.

3. La Posada Terrace: For budget tourists visiting Austin, the La Posada Terrace provides pleasant yet affordable lodging beginning at $89 per night. The poolside lounge and picnic area are available to guests.

4. Drury Inn & Suites Houston Near the Galleria: Enjoy a pleasant stay in Houston at the Drury Inn & Suites, where rates start at only $101/night. The facilities at this pet-friendly hotel include a pool, complimentary Wi-Fi, and a fitness center.

5. America's Best Value Inn & Suites: With rates starting at $59 a night, this budget motel in San Antonio provides a comfortable stay with basic amenities such as free Wi-Fi, parking, and a fitness center.

6. Focus Hotel Dallas North: This budget hotel offers decent accommodations starting at $80 per night without sacrificing service. Guests may use the fitness facility and business amenities on-site.

7. Holiday Inn Express & Suites Conroe: This affordable hotel in Conroe starts at $94 per night. Guests may make use of the daily breakfast, heated pool, and free Wi-Fi.

The services, facilities, pricing, and location of the two types of hotels differ. Luxury hotels are often more costly, feature higher-end rooms, and superior facilities, and are located in more upmarket neighborhoods. Budget hotels often provide fewer services and facilities and are located in more cheap places.

CHAPTER 8

ANTIQUES AND THRIFT SHOPS

Texas is a great state to explore for antique and thrift shopping opportunities. With its wonderful variety of shops and stores, it is no surprise that shopping for vintage and pre-owned items is a favorite pastime of many Texans. From larger stores like Goodwill to small boutiques specializing in pre-loved items, there is something to suit all tastes and budgets.

In this chapter, we will explore some of the best antique and thrift shopping destinations in Texas and share tips on how to get the best bargains. So come along on this journey into the wonderful world of vintage shopping in Texas– we guarantee you won't be disappointed!

I'm not afraid to admit that some of my favorite clothes are Goodwill finds. Why spend outrageous prices for something as insignificant as clothing when you can obtain equivalent fashions for a fraction of the price? That being said, Texas is brimming with fantastic thrift and antique stores where you can score excellent deals on anything from clothing to furniture to vintage knick-knacks.

Dallas Thrift Giant

Everything in this store is color-coded by price, making combing through the limitless possibilities less overwhelming. Many of the things, from high thread count sheets to designer handbags, are also of great quality. Why wouldn't you if you could obtain excellent products for a fraction of the price? Furthermore, there are various sites around the state, so if you visit more than one, you'll have plenty of options.

Thrift Town, Austin

This is the jackpot if you're searching for an enhanced Goodwill for bargain shopping in Texas. You'll discover fantastic prices on shoes, designer purses, clothing, and just much everything else your heart desires. They often have big sales during the holidays, and if you become a VIP member, you can get discounts. Additional sites may be found in Dallas and San Antonio.

The Cottage Shop, Houston

The Cottage Shop, well known for its clothes assortment, is full of one-of-a-kind items, both modern and old. Their shoe collection is especially impressive, and all sales benefit The Women's Home, so you can feel good about yourself for helping a good cause.

Lula B's, Dallas

The products here aren't inexpensive, but they are uncommon and will undoubtedly transport you back in time. Who knows what type of treasures you'll unearth, from antique diner seats to vintage lamps?

Uncommon Objects - Austin

Uncommon Objects, Austin's most famous antique shop/thrift store, is noted for its abundance of oddities and unpredictability. You didn't spend enough time looking if you didn't come up with at least one thing.

Curiosities -Dallas

You'll have a great time looking over everything here. From odd antiquities to enormous artworks and everything in between, you might easily lose track of time perusing. Like many antique shops, the pricing on certain goods isn't the cheapest, but the quality is unrivaled.

Feathers Boutique in Austin

This one's for the ladies. Feathers is a vintage women's clothes and shoe store that dates from the 1920s through the 1990s. So, whether you're planning a costume party or just want to give yourself a dose of nostalgia now and again, you should go check out this fantastic location.

And a lot more...

CHAPTER 9

IMPORTANT TIPS

Texas is packed full of fantastic activities, attractions and experiences for you to enjoy on your vacation. In this chapter, we will provide you with some basic tips to help you navigate your way around the Lone Star State and make the most of your trip. Get ready to explore Texas in style!

- Take Public Transportation

Texas is a large state, and taking a cab across it would be prohibitively expensive. It is strongly advised to make use of the various public transportation options available across the state. The metro and the bus are two of the greatest methods to go about the state. Traveling via public transportation will reduce the cost of your journey and so help you save money.

- Be Nice and Expect Conversations

If you're from a big city, you could be wary when people establish prolonged eye contact. Let your guard down in Texas; people are friendly, and it's rare not to say hi to strangers. You may also anticipate the door to be held open for you, and the person assisting you at the gas station will truly inquire how you are - and it is impolite if you do not reciprocate.

- Keep an Eye Out For Critters.

Texas is home to creatures and insects that you may have never seen before. While rattlesnakes are the most well-known, keep an eye out for cougars, enormous scorpions, tarantulas, spiders, and fire ants as well. Wild pigs, who normally avoid humans but may be highly hostile when confronted, are among the most terrifying creatures you might meet.

- It's Referred to as a Coke.

When you go to the South, the "soda" vs. "pop" discussion takes an interesting turn. Everything in Texas is a "Coke," whether it's a Sprite, Dr. Pepper, or Fanta. Of course, when dining out, it's best to order by brand name. If you're at a friend's house and want something bubbly, they'll normally ask "What kind" if you indicate you want a Coke.

- Avoid Rush Hour

You don't have to worry about traffic if you're driving along a gravel road in West Texas. If you're visiting any of Texas' main cities, such as Dallas, Austin, Houston, or San Antonio, you should plan on sitting in traffic between 8 a.m. and 5 p.m. Above all, avoid I-35 as much as possible; the Texas Department of Transportation has even erected signs joking about how the route is generally despised for its ongoing construction.

- Guns Are Permitted

Don't be alarmed if you see a pistol holstered on a passerby's hips; firearms are almost encouraged here. Professors at the University of Texas have resigned in protest of the campus carry law, which permits weapons on campus. Open carry is even permitted in Texas' public mental facilities. These kinds of regulations are now provoking a lot of controversy in the state legislature, with 40 gun proposals submitted in the 2017 legislative session alone.

- Avoid Particular Periods

Be aware of important events taking place in the areas you wish to visit, as they might drastically disrupt your vacation. Every March, over 300,000 travelers rush to Austin for SXSW, driving up lodging rates and packing practically every restaurant and tourist destination. South Padre Island is a popular undergraduate spring break destination, so unless you like body shots, stay away from this region in March and April.

- Don't Support Any Non-Texas Football Teams, Particularly Oklahoma

Football is incredibly important in Texas, especially at the high school level. It's one thing to run across a fan of a different Texas college than you, but it's quite another to run into someone shouting about their love of Oklahoma, which will quickly get you excluded. Seriously. Do not attempt it.

- The TABC is stringent

The Texas Alcohol Beverage Commission is notorious for its strictness. Without special late-night permission, bars cannot sell alcohol after midnight on weeknights. If a business wants to sell alcohol with brunch, they must first give the individual food or face a fine. TABC officials will conduct random and covert investigations into venues and punish them for over-serving customers or even if a brawl breaks out due to drunkenness. If you're a minor, don't even try it since they'll catch you.

CONCLUSION

Texas is a great place to visit if you are looking for a truly unique and memorable vacation experience. It is a haven for outdoor enthusiasts, food-loving travelers, and those who just want a chance to get away from the hustle and bustle of daily life. Whether you're planning on visiting a few of the cities, taking a road trip out west, or just taking your time to explore this diverse and beautiful state, there are many ways to enjoy a trip to Texas.

For those looking to explore the natural beauty of the Lone Star State, outdoor activities in Texas offer a lot of excitement. From hiking and camping to mountain biking and rock climbing, you'll find a variety of ways to get in touch with nature. You can also explore the many state parks for a chance to get up close and personal with the wildlife and unique landscapes of the region.

Texas is also a great place to experience some truly memorable culinary experiences. From savory Tex-Mex cuisine to signature steakhouse favorites, the state's rich culinary traditions are sure to satisfy any food-lover. There are also many barbecue joints scattered throughout the state offering up some of the best slow-cooked smoky meat around. And with so many excellent craft breweries and wineries, you'll have plenty of wonderful drinks to try.

Finally, there are many cultural attractions to enjoy all throughout the state. Museums, galleries, live music, theaters, and performing arts venues all provide a chance for travelers to get to know the local culture and history. There are also plenty of shops and boutiques around for those looking to pick up souvenirs or do some local shopping.

Whether you're looking for a relaxing vacation or an active adventure, a trip to Texas has something for everyone. With so much to explore and experience, you'll be sure to create some life-long memories. To ensure that your trip to Texas goes smoothly, be sure to book accommodations and activities in advance, prepare for any extreme weather conditions, and bring plenty of sunscreen and hats for maximum sun protection. Enjoy your time in the Lone Star State!

Printed in Great Britain
by Amazon